Your MONEYDATE journal

MICHELLE COOPER

STOKE Publishing

ISBN: 978-1-988675-22-0

Praise for …

"Your MoneyDate Journal keeps me balanced and at ease with the flow of my money. I am consciously aware of where we are with our money priorities for our family. What I love most of all is the ease I feel about money and the sense of contentment it allows in receiving our financial abundance." Heather Ruth

"I was immediately hooked by this simple and smart technique at money management and awareness. My MoneyDates have become a ritual for me as part of my weekly business planning. I am eager to open my bank accounts now. I am able to catch challenges before they happen and take the time to celebrate every win! I know that by focussing each week, I am inviting more and more to celebrate." Joy Kingsborough

"As an artist, I love creating a new reality… But when it came to the financial side of my career it wasn't helping me AT ALL in my business. Michelle's honest delivery, wicked humour, and jolts back into financial reality were just what I needed and Your MoneyDate Journal was a vital part of the process. I am creating a positive relationship with money, making money dates and keeping track of where I am and what I can do, and looking forward to the future of my business in a way I did not think possible." Erin Foggoa

"Your MoneyDate Journal has helped me immensely, not only in my personal life but in my business as well. My bills are all paid on time, I know what is coming in and what's going out every week. I actually look forward to my MoneyDate every single time because it makes me feel calm and in control when it comes to my money. No longer is money a guessing game. I used to absolutely detest running my numbers, so it would never happen. Now, I look forward to it." Cindy. VA

Dedication

This journal is dedicated to Joy and Meagan, who, when they saw my own rag tag version of this, jumped up and down and asked me to create this for them and the world. You have given me the idea, the encouragement and the support that I have needed along this journey. I'm grateful.

This journal is dedicated to Amy, Cindy and Steph, who continue to rave about this process and showed me that I could teach it to others. They prove to me consistently that it works. I'm grateful.

This journal is dedicated to Nick, Holly, Ostara and Tyr, who laugh with me, and at me, as I move through change and experience new things. I'm grateful.

This journal is dedicated to my higher power, the Universe, my inner cosmos and my intuition – I have all I need inside me.

I'm grateful.

Introduction

Welcome to Your MoneyDate Journal, you found us! What the heck is a MoneyDate, you may be asking?

A MoneyDate is a weekly date with your money – showing up and paying attention to the money in your life. This is a journal and planner which helps you get more money flowing into your life, hold yourself accountable to your vision and achieve abundance.

I'm excited that you have made the decision to become an active co-creator with your money. You are on the edge of a very exciting climb upwards in wealth. Inside this book, you will document your weekly date with your money, logging all the facts and figures as well as your feelings about where you are now and where you are heading. This is an amazing place to be, and I hope you're as excited as I am.

The MoneyDate Journal builds on the framework of my other book, **_Confessions of a Money Rock Star_**, supporting your journey to wealth and the abundance that is waiting for you.

We break down your work into weekly dates, monthly reviews, quarterly check-ins and journaling every step of the way. This process is based on how I have grown my own wealth and money mindset, and continue to move into ever increasing up-levels of abundance.

Amazing things are about to happen, so enjoy the ride and really dig in deep to this process. I invite you to make your MoneyDate count; make it a priority in your life. When we prioritize our money, we shine a spotlight on it and we are able to call in more- often more than we thought possible.

Money Dates are about achieving your money goals through momentum and change. It's totally doable for everyone. There's no secret, there's no luck involved, and there's no magic potion. There are things to work through, beliefs to shift and there's your action – your MoneyDate.

Michelle Cooper

Orientation to your Money Date Planner

WELCOME, MONEY ROCK STAR

This is not a traditional planner. This is a MONEY planner – a weekly appointment that you are having with your money that supports your commitment to growing your wealth and living an ever-increasing abundant life.

Use it every single week. Record all your balances – the good, the bad and the ugly.

Record how you feel and your goals and challenges. At the end of the month, use the Monthly Wrap Up pages. Let's see how far you have come! At the end of three months, use the Quarterly Review pages. Look at that momentum!

Join the MoneyDate Facebook Community. This is a place where we do MoneyDates together – live and in person. Connect with others who are changing their lives through this work. Join the Money Momentum Gang. Dig in, go deep and enjoy YOUR journey.

LINK: https://www.facebook.com/groups/MoneyDate/

Let's Get This Party Started

Creating awareness and accountability around our money shows it the attention it craves and desires. We also create the energy that attracts more money into our lives by spending time in gratitude and recognition. Like the fans at a rock concert, your money wants your undivided attention at regular intervals – it needs it, or it will find another rock star to become obsessed with and you will be left in the dust like some tired old former super star that is now singing in some dive bar in Reno.

Having a weekly money date where you check the balances on all your accounts – banks, credit cards and online resources like PayPal supports the growth of your money. Also, check how much is owed to you and how much you owe others. This is the all-encompassing view of your money, what comes in, what goes out and what hangs around. A great tool for awareness, this action step also builds your money rituals, otherwise known as "habits', but "ritual" sounds more kick-ass rockstar! Setting your priorities each week around your money will move you in a forward momentum and take control of where your money comes from and goes to, and it is incredibly empowering.

If your bestie called you and asked you for your time, would you put it off? Would you hesitate? I sure as heck wouldn't, because my bestie is important to me. I'd get that time in my schedule NOW. And if they said, "Hey rock star, let's do this every week!" it would become a non-negotiable date in my schedule. Make a commitment to your money, a scheduled time - set aside one hour each week to hang out with your money. If possible, make it the same day and time each week. It is non-negotiable- rain or shine, it happens. It is your date with your fan, your bestie, your abundance.

When that date comes up, you need access to information! You need access to bank accounts, credit card accounts and your business bookkeeping system- wherever you store all this awesome stuff. Don't plan to do your money date at the beach if you don't have access to the info you need on your phone. Set yourself up for success – Your MoneyDate Journal is where you record this information, a drink you enjoy, some awesome music playing – this is a date, so treat it as such.

Money is part of a Universal cycle – it flows both to you and away from you, and you are not only a part of that cycle, you are a participant in it. Money flows to you, perhaps from different sources, perhaps at different times of the month, but it's always flowing to you. Money that you have or is owed to you is commonly referred to as your ASSETS. Yup, you have them. They may be big or small but you have them. We look at three main areas:

• Bank accounts
• Accounts Receivable – money owed to you (this could be business or personal loans)
• Other places you are holding money like PayPal, gift cards or prepaid cards

Go through all your accounts and write out the balances – chequing, savings, PayPal.

Let's talk Accounts Receivable. This is the money that is owed to you for services you have provided in your business or money that is owed to you because you lent it out to someone. Maybe you lent money to your broke-ass brother – that's an account receivable as much as a client who you created a website for whom has yet to pay you for services rendered. You can find this information in your bookkeeping software or even better, ask your bookkeeper. However, I invite you to think about why people owe you money. How much is it? When are they going to pay you? How do you collect money from clients or your customers? Do you accept credit cards? If you don't, you may as well be living in the dark ages. Get that money in your bank account – if your price can't absorb 2-3% processing fees, then you have bigger problems. Seek advice from a professional.

Take Action People! Action-Jackson Gets Shit Done! What are you going to do to collect money that is owed to you? What are your priorities for your money? Write this down.

Hold yourself accountable. Now, how do your assets make you feel? Write in your journal about this. Pause for a moment and sit with it. Close your eyes, and identify where in your body you feel this and what your body is telling you about the feeling. Journal, journal, journal!

The second half of the money cycle is money that flows away from you. In a healthy cycle, the money that flows away from you feels good! You receive a bill, you are grateful for the service or product that the bill provided and so you are ecstatic to pay that bill. Be ecstatic, be grateful, be in as high a vibration in the outflow of money as you are in the inflow of money. Sometimes we spend money we don't have yet, we borrow money or we use credit facilities to complete transactions. These are your LIABILITIES – the money you owe. This includes your:

- Credit cards
- Loans
- Accounts payable

Check all your credit card and loan balances. Write them down in detail. Note when payment is due.

What the heck are accounts payable, you may be asking? It is services or products that you have received, and now you have a bill for them, but you haven't yet paid for it. Let's say you owe money to someone – be that the electric company, your bookkeeper, or your friend who lent you $50 at the last home party you went to, because you just had to have that thingy majig. That is an account payable. If you're in business, you can get an accounts payable report from your bookkeeping software or your bookkeeper.

Remember Action Jackson? Here she comes again to take action. What are you going to do right now or in the next seven days to pay these liabilities? What money do you need to move around? What are some upcoming expenses that you should be budgeting for? Prepare ahead of time. When we don't prepare, we use our credit card and we are then in debt! Don't do that! Prepare for expenses.

And of course, we need to talk to ourselves about this – fortunately, we have that handy thing called journaling we've been practicing. How does your deadline date make you feel? How can you improve your situation? What are your money affirmations this week? What is your Money Alignment Statement? Are you in alignment with your money? What are you grateful for in regards to money right now?

Always seal this process with gratitude. Remember, one thing you're grateful for and three reasons why.

The Purse Strings

What does your wallet look like? Would a pick-pocket give it back? Is it a rag-tag mess of receipts, cards and miscellaneous items? Do you have items in there that don't relate to money? Oops, I think there may be a cigarette in there from 20 years ago! When you open it, are you nervous about what may or may not fall out? Would CSI be able to identify you and where you have been by your wallet?

Your wallet's purpose is to hold your money. It's simple. It doesn't contain your phone, your passport or your stash. It contains your money and items associated with your money like your Citrine (more on that in the Money Rock Star book), your credit cards, your chequebook (yeah, they still make those things) and your bank cards. Cleaning out your wallet creates a sacred space for your money to live and thrive. I'm not saying that you need to iron your dollar bills, well, maybe I am, but if that doesn't jive with you, that's okay.

The way you keep your money gives the Universe a sign as to whether or not you're ready for your fortune to multiply. Make sure your bills are neatly arranged in your wallet or it is in some kind of order. De-clutter it and get rid of the trash you no longer need such as receipts, etc. Reverence for your cash will go a long way. Your wallet should say something about you. What does yours say? Does it say that you're a homeless hobo living on the railroad, or does it say you are a rock star?

Can your bank account accept money in different forms? By electronic means, credit card, bank machine, and just plain cash? Is there a limit to how much you can deposit? Here's a funny historical fact about money. Many years ago, when lotteries were just beginning, many accounts wouldn't allow the winners to deposit their winnings as they couldn't handle that amount of money. Of course, they fixed that, but every lottery winner is now provided with an optional advisor to help them "manage" the flow of money.

Resources

I am here for you and am so pleased to provide you with some extra support.   This comes to you via a private Facebook Community, just for you and others on the same journey. If you're a spreadsheet kinda gal – there's spreadsheets, graphs and all the bells and whistles.

Need some headspace? There are guided money meditations, just for you.

Want some further support and motivation? There is an invitation to The Vault, Michelle's private Facebook community for all things money!

Are you interested in going further with this work? Michelle offers a course that walks you through the MoneyDate, step by step. Michelle walks alongside you as go through the process, asking thought provoking questions that help you go deeper and move into abundance even faster. For those who want to catch the express train to money, you may want to check out Your MoneyDate Course.

The Vault - Facebook Group
https://www.facebook.com/groups/thebusinessvault/

Your MoneyDate - Facebook Group
https://www.facebook.com/groups/MoneyDate/

Grab the MoneyDate Bonuses!
https://michellebcooper.com/money-date-bonuses

Date: _____

Assets

Chequing _____

Savings _____

Other _____

Paypal _____

Accounts Receivable

   Current (0-30 Days) _____

   31-60 Days _____

   61+ Days _____

Action Steps to Collect Money This Week

_____

_____

_____

_____

_____

_____

Priorities for Cash Flow

What will I do with the money I receive?

_____

_____

_____

_____

_____

_____

Date: _____

Liabilities

Credit Card _____

Credit Card _____

Other _____

Loan _____

Accounts Payable _____

Current (0-30 Days) _____

31-60 Days _____

61+ Days _____

Action Steps to Release Money This Week

What bills will I pay?

_____

_____

_____

_____

_____

_____

Upcoming Expenses to Prepare For

_____

_____

_____

_____

_____

_____

Date: _____

Journaling & Notes

How does the big picture of my money make me feel today?

_____
_____
_____
_____
_____
_____

How can I improve my situation?

_____
_____
_____
_____
_____
_____

My money affirmation for this week...

_____
_____
_____
_____
_____
_____

I am grateful for

Your
MONEYDATE
journal

Date: _____

Assets

Chequing _____

Savings _____

Other _____

Paypal _____

Accounts Receivable _____

Current (0-30 Days) _____

31-60 Days _____

61+ Days _____

Action Steps to Collect Money This Week

_____

_____

_____

_____

_____

_____

Priorities for Cash Flow

What will I do with the money I receive?

_____

_____

_____

_____

_____

_____

Date: _____

Liabilities

Credit Card _____

Credit Card _____

Other _____

Loan _____

Accounts Payable _____

Current (0-30 Days) _____

31-60 Days _____

61+ Days _____

Action Steps to Release Money This Week

What bills will I pay?

_____

_____

_____

_____

_____

_____

Upcoming Expenses to Prepare For

_____

_____

_____

_____

_____

Date: _____

Journaling & Notes

How does the big picture of my money make me feel today?

_____

_____

_____

_____

_____

_____

How can I improve my situation?

_____

_____

_____

_____

_____

_____

My money affirmation for this week...

_____

_____

_____

_____

_____

_____

I am grateful for

_____
_____
_____
_____
_____
_____
_____
_____
_____
_____
_____
_____
_____
_____
_____
_____
_____
_____
_____
_____
_____
_____
_____
_____
_____
_____
_____
_____

Your MONEYDATE journal

Date: _____

Assets

Chequing _____

Savings _____

Other _____

Paypal _____

Accounts Receivable _____

Current (0-30 Days) _____

31-60 Days _____

61+ Days _____

Action Steps to Collect Money This Week

_____

_____

_____

_____

_____

_____

Priorities for Cash Flow

What will I do with the money I receive?

_____

_____

_____

_____

_____

Your
MONEYDATE
journal

Date: _____

Liabilities

Credit Card _____

Credit Card _____

Other _____

Loan _____

Accounts Payable _____

    Current (0-30 Days) _____

    31-60 Days _____

    61+ Days _____

Action Steps to Release Money This Week

What bills will I pay?

_____

_____

_____

_____

_____

_____

Upcoming Expenses to Prepare For

_____

_____

_____

_____

_____

_____

Date: _____

Journaling & Notes

How does the big picture of my money make me feel today?

_____
_____
_____
_____
_____
_____

How can I improve my situation?

_____
_____
_____
_____
_____

My money affirmation for this week...

_____
_____
_____
_____
_____

I am grateful for

Your
MONEYDATE
journal

Date: _____

Assets

Chequing _____

Savings _____

Other _____

Paypal _____

Accounts Receivable _____

    Current (0-30 Days) _____

    31-60 Days _____

    61+ Days _____

Action Steps to Collect Money This Week

_____

_____

_____

_____

_____

_____

Priorities for Cash Flow

What will I do with the money I receive?

_____

_____

_____

_____

_____

_____

Date: _____

Liabilities

Credit Card _____

Credit Card _____

Other _____

Loan _____

Accounts Payable _____

    Current (0-30 Days) _____

    31-60 Days _____

    61+ Days _____

Action Steps to Release Money This Week

What bills will I pay?

_____

_____

_____

_____

_____

_____

Upcoming Expenses to Prepare For

_____

_____

_____

_____

_____

_____

Date: _____

Journaling & Notes

How does the big picture of my money make me feel today?

_____

_____

_____

_____

_____

How can I improve my situation?

_____

_____

_____

_____

_____

My money affirmation for this week...

_____

_____

_____

_____

_____

I am grateful for

Date: _____

REFLECTION

What are you most proud of achieving?	Did you remain in alignment with your money?
What milestones did you bust through? Which ones need to be adjusted?	How did you reward yourself?
Where did you drop the ball? How can you prevent that from happening in the future?	How do you feel about the month overall?

Money talks.
I listen.

Your MONEYDATE journal

Date: _____

Assets

Chequing _____

Savings _____

Other _____

Paypal _____

Accounts Receivable _____

    Current (0-30 Days) _____

    31-60 Days _____

    61+ Days _____

Action Steps to Collect Money This Week

_____

_____

_____

_____

_____

_____

Priorities for Cash Flow

What will I do with the money I receive?

_____

_____

_____

_____

_____

_____

Date: _____

Liabilities

Credit Card _____

Credit Card _____

Other _____

Loan _____

Accounts Payable _____

    Current (0-30 Days) _____

    31-60 Days _____

    61+ Days _____

Action Steps to Release Money This Week

What bills will I pay?

_____

_____

_____

_____

_____

_____

Upcoming Expenses to Prepare For

_____

_____

_____

_____

_____

_____

Date: _____

Journaling & Notes

How does the big picture of my money make me feel today?

_____
_____
_____
_____
_____
_____

How can I improve my situation?

_____
_____
_____
_____
_____
_____

My money affirmation for this week...

_____
_____
_____
_____
_____
_____

I am grateful for

Date: _____

Assets

Chequing _____

Savings _____

Other _____

Paypal _____

Accounts Receivable _____

    Current (0-30 Days) _____

    31-60 Days _____

    61+ Days _____

Action Steps to Collect Money This Week

_____

_____

_____

_____

_____

_____

Priorities for Cash Flow

What will I do with the money I receive?

_____

_____

_____

_____

_____

Your MONEY DATE journal

Date: _____

Liabilities

<u>Credit Card</u> _____

<u>Credit Card</u> _____

<u>Other</u> _____

<u>Loan</u> _____

<u>Accounts Payable</u> _____

    <u>Current (0-30 Days)</u> _____

    <u>31-60 Days</u> _____

    <u>61+ Days</u> _____

Action Steps to Release Money This Week

What bills will I pay?

_____

_____

_____

_____

_____

_____

Upcoming Expenses to Prepare For

_____

_____

_____

_____

_____

_____

Your MONEYDATE journal

Date: _____

Journaling & Notes

How does the big picture of my money make me feel today?

_____
_____
_____
_____
_____
_____

How can I improve my situation?

_____
_____
_____
_____
_____
_____

My money affirmation for this week...

_____
_____
_____
_____
_____
_____

I am grateful for

Date: _____

Assets

Chequing _____

Savings _____

Other _____

Paypal _____

Accounts Receivable

Current (0-30 Days) _____

31-60 Days _____

61+ Days _____

Action Steps to Collect Money This Week

_____

_____

_____

_____

_____

_____

Priorities for Cash Flow

What will I do with the money I receive?

_____

_____

_____

_____

_____

Your MONEYDATE journal

Date: _____

Liabilities

Credit Card _____

Credit Card _____

Other _____

Loan _____

Accounts Payable _____

Current (0-30 Days) _____

31-60 Days _____

61+ Days _____

Action Steps to Release Money This Week

What bills will I pay?

_____

_____

_____

_____

_____

_____

Upcoming Expenses to Prepare For

_____

_____

_____

_____

_____

Your
MONEYDATE
journal

Date: _____

Journaling & Notes

How does the big picture of my money make me feel today?

_____
_____
_____
_____
_____
_____

How can I improve my situation?

_____
_____
_____
_____
_____
_____

My money affirmation for this week...

_____
_____
_____
_____
_____
_____

I am grateful for

Your
MONEYDATE *journal*

Date: _____

Assets

Chequing _____

Savings _____

Other _____

Paypal _____

Accounts Receivable

    Current (0-30 Days) _____

    31-60 Days _____

    61+ Days _____

Action Steps to Collect Money This Week

_____

_____

_____

_____

_____

_____

Priorities for Cash Flow

What will I do with the money I receive?

_____

_____

_____

_____

_____

_____

Your
MONEYDATE
journal

Date: _____

Liabilities

Credit Card _____

Credit Card _____

Other _____

Loan _____

Accounts Payable _____

   Current (0-30 Days) _____

   31-60 Days _____

   61+ Days _____

Action Steps to Release Money This Week

What bills will I pay?

_____

_____

_____

_____

_____

_____

Upcoming Expenses to Prepare For

_____

_____

_____

_____

_____

_____

Date: _____

Journaling & Notes

How does the big picture of my money make me feel today?

_____
_____
_____
_____
_____
_____

How can I improve my situation?

_____
_____
_____
_____
_____
_____

My money affirmation for this week...

_____
_____
_____
_____
_____
_____

I am grateful for

_____
_____
_____
_____
_____
_____
_____
_____
_____
_____
_____
_____
_____
_____
_____
_____
_____
_____
_____
_____
_____
_____
_____
_____
_____
_____
_____
_____

Date: _____

REFLECTION

What are you most proud of achieving?	Did you remain in alignment with your money?
What milestones did you bust through? Which ones need to be adjusted?	How did you reward yourself?
Where did you drop the ball? How can you prevent that from happening in the future?	How do you feel about the month overall?

Money flows to me easily and consistently.

Your
MONEYDATE *journal*

Date: _____

Assets

Chequing _____

Savings _____

Other _____

Paypal _____

Accounts Receivable _____

    Current (0-30 Days) _____

    31-60 Days _____

    61+ Days _____

Action Steps to Collect Money This Week

_____

_____

_____

_____

_____

_____

Priorities for Cash Flow

What will I do with the money I receive?

_____

_____

_____

_____

_____

_____

Your
MONEYDATE
journal

Date: _____

Liabilities

Credit Card _____

Credit Card _____

Other _____

Loan _____

Accounts Payable _____

    Current (0-30 Days) _____

    31-60 Days _____

    61+ Days _____

Action Steps to Release Money This Week

What bills will I pay?

_____

_____

_____

_____

_____

_____

Upcoming Expenses to Prepare For

_____

_____

_____

_____

_____

_____

Date: _____

Journaling & Notes

How does the big picture of my money make me feel today?

_____
_____
_____
_____
_____
_____

How can I improve my situation?

_____
_____
_____
_____
_____
_____

My money affirmation for this week...

_____
_____
_____
_____
_____
_____

I am grateful for

_____
_____
_____
_____
_____
_____
_____
_____
_____
_____
_____
_____
_____
_____
_____
_____
_____
_____
_____
_____
_____
_____
_____
_____
_____
_____
_____
_____

Date: _____

Assets

Chequing _____

Savings _____

Other _____

Paypal _____

Accounts Receivable _____

Current (0-30 Days) _____

31-60 Days _____

61+ Days _____

Action Steps to Collect Money This Week

_____

_____

_____

_____

_____

_____

Priorities for Cash Flow

What will I do with the money I receive?

_____

_____

_____

_____

_____

Date: _____

Liabilities

Credit Card _____

Credit Card _____

Other _____

Loan _____

Accounts Payable _____

    Current (0-30 Days) _____

    31-60 Days _____

    61+ Days _____

Action Steps to Release Money This Week

What bills will I pay?

_____

_____

_____

_____

_____

_____

Upcoming Expenses to Prepare For

_____

_____

_____

_____

_____

_____

Date: _____

Journaling & Notes

How does the big picture of my money make me feel today?

_____

_____

_____

_____

_____

_____

How can I improve my situation?

_____

_____

_____

_____

_____

_____

My money affirmation for this week...

_____

_____

_____

_____

_____

_____

I am grateful for

Your MONEYDATE journal

Date: _____

Assets

Chequing _____

Savings _____

Other _____

Paypal _____

Accounts Receivable _____

Current (0-30 Days) _____

31-60 Days _____

61+ Days _____

Action Steps to Collect Money This Week

_____

_____

_____

_____

_____

_____

Priorities for Cash Flow

What will I do with the money I receive?

_____

_____

_____

_____

_____

_____

Date: _____

Liabilities

Credit Card _____

Credit Card _____

Other _____

Loan _____

Accounts Payable _____

    Current (0-30 Days) _____

    31-60 Days _____

    61+ Days _____

Action Steps to Release Money This Week

What bills will I pay?
_____
_____
_____
_____
_____
_____

Upcoming Expenses to Prepare For

_____
_____
_____
_____
_____
_____

Date: _____

Journaling & Notes

How does the big picture of my money make me feel today?

_____

_____

_____

_____

_____

_____

How can I improve my situation?

_____

_____

_____

_____

_____

_____

My money affirmation for this week...

_____

_____

_____

_____

_____

_____

I am grateful for

_____
_____
_____
_____
_____
_____
_____
_____
_____
_____
_____
_____
_____
_____
_____
_____
_____
_____
_____
_____
_____
_____
_____
_____
_____
_____
_____
_____

Your MONEYDATE journal

Date: _____

Assets

Chequing _____

Savings _____

Other _____

Paypal _____

Accounts Receivable _____

Current (0-30 Days) _____

31-60 Days _____

61+ Days _____

Action Steps to Collect Money This Week

_____
_____
_____
_____
_____
_____

Priorities for Cash Flow

What will I do with the money I receive?

_____
_____
_____
_____
_____
_____

Your
MONEYDATE
journal

Date: _____

Liabilities

Credit Card _____

Credit Card _____

Other _____

Loan _____

Accounts Payable _____

Current (0-30 Days) _____

31-60 Days _____

61+ Days _____

Action Steps to Release Money This Week

What bills will I pay?

_____

_____

_____

_____

_____

_____

Upcoming Expenses to Prepare For

_____

_____

_____

_____

_____

_____

Your
MONEYDATE
journal

Date: _____

Journaling & Notes

How does the big picture of my money make me feel today?

_____
_____
_____
_____
_____

How can I improve my situation?

_____
_____
_____
_____
_____

My money affirmation for this week...

_____
_____
_____
_____
_____

I am grateful for

Date: _____

REFLECTION

What are you most proud of achieving?	Did you remain in alignment with your money?
What milestones did you bust through? Which ones need to be adjusted?	How did you reward yourself?
Where did you drop the ball? How can you prevent that from happening in the future?	How do you feel about the month overall?

I trust that more money is on its way to me.

Date: _____

What was your goal for the end of the quarter?

_____
_____
_____
_____
_____
_____

Did you achieve it? What percentage? (divide the actual by the goal $)

_____
_____
_____

How do you feel about your money right now?

_____
_____
_____
_____
_____
_____

What would you like to change or shift?

_____
_____
_____
_____
_____
_____

What can you do to support that change or shift?

_____
_____
_____
_____
_____
_____
_____
_____

What is your goal for the next three months?

_____
_____
_____
_____
_____
_____
_____
_____
_____
_____
_____

Your
MONEYDATE
journal

Date: _____

Assets

Chequing _____

Savings _____

Other _____

Paypal _____

Accounts Receivable _____

Current (0-30 Days) _____

31-60 Days _____

61+ Days _____

Action Steps to Collect Money This Week

_____

_____

_____

_____

_____

_____

Priorities for Cash Flow

What will I do with the money I receive?

_____

_____

_____

_____

_____

_____

Date: _____

Liabilities

Credit Card _____

Credit Card _____

Other _____

Loan _____

Accounts Payable _____

Current (0-30 Days) _____

31-60 Days _____

61+ Days _____

Action Steps to Release Money This Week

What bills will I pay?

_____

_____

_____

_____

_____

_____

Upcoming Expenses to Prepare For

_____

_____

_____

_____

_____

_____

Your MONEY DATE journal

Date: _____

Journaling & Notes

How does the big picture of my money make me feel today?

_____
_____
_____
_____
_____
_____

How can I improve my situation?

_____
_____
_____
_____
_____
_____

My money affirmation for this week...

_____
_____
_____
_____
_____
_____

I am grateful for

Your MONEY DATE journal

Date: _____

Assets

Chequing _____

Savings _____

Other _____

Paypal _____

Accounts Receivable _____

Current (0-30 Days) _____

31-60 Days _____

61+ Days _____

Action Steps to Collect Money This Week

_____

_____

_____

_____

_____

_____

Priorities for Cash Flow

What will I do with the money I receive?

_____

_____

_____

_____

_____

_____

Your
MONEY DATE
journal

Date: _____

Liabilities

Credit Card _____

Credit Card _____

Other _____

Loan _____

Accounts Payable _____

    Current (0-30 Days) _____

    31-60 Days _____

    61+ Days _____

Action Steps to Release Money This Week

What bills will I pay?

_____

_____

_____

_____

_____

_____

Upcoming Expenses to Prepare For

_____

_____

_____

_____

_____

Your MONEYDATE journal

Date: _____

Journaling & Notes

How does the big picture of my money make me feel today?

_____
_____
_____
_____
_____
_____

How can I improve my situation?

_____
_____
_____
_____
_____
_____

My money affirmation for this week...

_____
_____
_____
_____
_____
_____

I am grateful for

Your MONEYDATE journal

Date: _____

Assets

Chequing _____

Savings _____

Other _____

Paypal _____

Accounts Receivable _____

Current (0-30 Days) _____

31-60 Days _____

61+ Days _____

Action Steps to Collect Money This Week

_____

_____

_____

_____

_____

_____

Priorities for Cash Flow

What will I do with the money I receive?

_____

_____

_____

_____

_____

_____

Date: _____

Liabilities

Credit Card _____

Credit Card _____

Other _____

Loan _____

Accounts Payable _____

Current (0-30 Days) _____

31-60 Days _____

61+ Days _____

Action Steps to Release Money This Week

What bills will I pay?

_____

_____

_____

_____

_____

_____

Upcoming Expenses to Prepare For

_____

_____

_____

_____

_____

_____

Your MONEYDATE journal

Date: _____

Journaling & Notes

How does the big picture of my money make me feel today?

_____
_____
_____
_____
_____
_____

How can I improve my situation?

_____
_____
_____
_____
_____
_____

My money affirmation for this week...

_____
_____
_____
_____
_____
_____

I am grateful for

Your
MONEYDATE *journal*

Date: _____

Assets

Chequing _____

Savings _____

Other _____

Paypal _____

Accounts Receivable _____

Current (0-30 Days) _____

31-60 Days _____

61+ Days _____

Action Steps to Collect Money This Week

_____

_____

_____

_____

_____

_____

Priorities for Cash Flow

What will I do with the money I receive?

_____

_____

_____

_____

_____

Your MONEYDATE journal

Date: _____

Liabilities

Credit Card _____

Credit Card _____

Other _____

Loan _____

Accounts Payable _____

Current (0-30 Days) _____

31-60 Days _____

61+ Days _____

Action Steps to Release Money This Week

What bills will I pay?

_____

_____

_____

_____

_____

_____

Upcoming Expenses to Prepare For

_____

_____

_____

_____

_____

_____

Date: _____

Journaling & Notes

How does the big picture of my money make me feel today?

_____

_____

_____

_____

_____

_____

How can I improve my situation?

_____

_____

_____

_____

_____

_____

My money affirmation for this week...

_____

_____

_____

_____

_____

_____

I am grateful for

_____
_____
_____
_____
_____
_____
_____
_____
_____
_____
_____
_____
_____
_____
_____
_____
_____
_____
_____
_____
_____
_____
_____
_____
_____
_____
_____

Date: _____

REFLECTION

What are you most proud of achieving?	Did you remain in alignment with your money?
What milestones did you bust through? Which ones need to be adjusted?	How did you reward yourself?
Where did you drop the ball? How can you prevent that from happening in the future?	How do you feel about the month overall?

I co-create money.

Your MONEYDATE journal

Date: _____

Assets

Chequing _____

Savings _____

Other _____

Paypal _____

Accounts Receivable _____

Current (0-30 Days) _____

31-60 Days _____

61+ Days _____

Action Steps to Collect Money This Week

_____

_____

_____

_____

_____

_____

Priorities for Cash Flow

What will I do with the money I receive?

_____

_____

_____

_____

_____

_____

Your
MONEYDATE
journal

Date: _____

Liabilities
Credit Card _____
Credit Card _____
Other _____
Loan _____
Accounts Payable _____

Current (0-30 Days) _____
31-60 Days _____
61+ Days _____

Action Steps to Release Money This Week
What bills will I pay?
_____
_____
_____
_____
_____
_____

Upcoming Expenses to Prepare For
_____
_____
_____
_____
_____
_____

Date: _____

Journaling & Notes

How does the big picture of my money make me feel today?

_____
_____
_____
_____
_____
_____

How can I improve my situation?

_____
_____
_____
_____
_____
_____

My money affirmation for this week...

_____
_____
_____
_____
_____
_____

I am grateful for

Your MONEY DATE journal

Date: _____

Assets

Chequing _____

Savings _____

Other _____

Paypal _____

Accounts Receivable

    Current (0-30 Days) _____

    31-60 Days _____

    61+ Days _____

Action Steps to Collect Money This Week

_____

_____

_____

_____

_____

_____

Priorities for Cash Flow

What will I do with the money I receive?

_____

_____

_____

_____

_____

_____

Your
MONEYDATE
journal

Date: _____

Liabilities

Credit Card _____

Credit Card _____

Other _____

Loan _____

Accounts Payable _____

Current (0-30 Days) _____

31-60 Days _____

61+ Days _____

Action Steps to Release Money This Week

What bills will I pay?
_____
_____
_____
_____
_____
_____

Upcoming Expenses to Prepare For

_____
_____
_____
_____
_____
_____

Date: _____

Journaling & Notes

How does the big picture of my money make me feel today?

_____

_____

_____

_____

_____

_____

How can I improve my situation?

_____

_____

_____

_____

_____

_____

My money affirmation for this week...

_____

_____

_____

_____

_____

_____

I am grateful for

Date: _____

Assets

Chequing _____

Savings _____

Other _____

Paypal _____

Accounts Receivable _____

Current (0-30 Days) _____

31-60 Days _____

61+ Days _____

Action Steps to Collect Money This Week

_____

_____

_____

_____

_____

_____

Priorities for Cash Flow

What will I do with the money I receive?

_____

_____

_____

_____

_____

_____

Date: _____

Liabilities

Credit Card _____

Credit Card _____

Other _____

Loan _____

Accounts Payable _____

Current (0-30 Days) _____

31-60 Days _____

61+ Days _____

Action Steps to Release Money This Week

What bills will I pay?

_____

_____

_____

_____

_____

_____

Upcoming Expenses to Prepare For

_____

_____

_____

_____

_____

_____

Your MONEYDATE *journal*

Date: _____

Journaling & Notes

How does the big picture of my money make me feel today?

_____
_____
_____
_____
_____
_____

How can I improve my situation?

_____
_____
_____
_____
_____
_____

My money affirmation for this week...

_____
_____
_____
_____
_____
_____

I am grateful for

Date: _____

Assets

Chequing _____

Savings _____

Other _____

Paypal _____

Accounts Receivable _____

Current (0-30 Days) _____

31-60 Days _____

61+ Days _____

Action Steps to Collect Money This Week

_____

_____

_____

_____

_____

_____

Priorities for Cash Flow

What will I do with the money I receive?

_____

_____

_____

_____

_____

_____

Date: _____

Liabilities

Credit Card _____

Credit Card _____

Other _____

Loan _____

Accounts Payable _____

    Current (0-30 Days) _____

    31-60 Days _____

    61+ Days _____

Action Steps to Release Money This Week

What bills will I pay?

_____

_____

_____

_____

_____

_____

Upcoming Expenses to Prepare For

_____

_____

_____

_____

_____

_____

Your
MONEYDATE
journal

Date: _____

Journaling & Notes

How does the big picture of my money make me feel today?

_____
_____
_____
_____
_____
_____

How can I improve my situation?

_____
_____
_____
_____
_____
_____

My money affirmation for this week...

_____
_____
_____
_____
_____
_____

I am grateful for

Date: _____

REFLECTION

What are you most proud of achieving?	Did you remain in alignment with your money?
What milestones did you bust through? Which ones need to be adjusted?	How did you reward yourself?
Where did you drop the ball? How can you prevent that from happening in the future?	How do you feel about the month overall?

I am grateful and overflowing in abundance.

Your MONEYDATE journal

Date: _____

Assets

Chequing _____

Savings _____

Other _____

Paypal _____

Accounts Receivable

Current (0-30 Days) _____

31-60 Days _____

61+ Days _____

Action Steps to Collect Money This Week

_____

_____

_____

_____

_____

_____

Priorities for Cash Flow

What will I do with the money I receive?

_____

_____

_____

_____

_____

_____

Date: _____

Liabilities

Credit Card _____

Credit Card _____

Other _____

Loan _____

Accounts Payable _____

Current (0-30 Days) _____

31-60 Days _____

61+ Days _____

Action Steps to Release Money This Week

What bills will I pay?

_____

_____

_____

_____

_____

_____

Upcoming Expenses to Prepare For

_____

_____

_____

_____

_____

_____

Date: _____

Journaling & Notes

How does the big picture of my money make me feel today?

_____
_____
_____
_____
_____
_____

How can I improve my situation?

_____
_____
_____
_____
_____
_____

My money affirmation for this week...

_____
_____
_____
_____
_____

I am grateful for

_____

_____

_____

_____

_____

_____

_____

_____

_____

_____

_____

_____

_____

_____

_____

_____

_____

_____

_____

_____

_____

_____

_____

_____

_____

_____

_____

_____

Your MONEYDATE journal

Date: _____

Assets

Chequing _____

Savings _____

Other _____

Paypal _____

Accounts Receivable _____

Current (0-30 Days) _____

31-60 Days _____

61+ Days _____

Action Steps to Collect Money This Week

_____

_____

_____

_____

_____

_____

Priorities for Cash Flow

What will I do with the money I receive?

_____

_____

_____

_____

_____

_____

Date: _____

Liabilities

Credit Card _____

Credit Card _____

Other _____

Loan _____

Accounts Payable _____

Current (0-30 Days) _____

31-60 Days _____

61+ Days _____

Action Steps to Release Money This Week

What bills will I pay?

_____

_____

_____

_____

_____

_____

Upcoming Expenses to Prepare For

_____

_____

_____

_____

_____

_____

Date: _____

Journaling & Notes

How does the big picture of my money make me feel today?

_____
_____
_____
_____
_____
_____

How can I improve my situation?

_____
_____
_____
_____
_____
_____

My money affirmation for this week...

_____
_____
_____
_____
_____
_____

I am grateful for

Your MONEYDATE journal

Date: _____

Assets

Chequing _____

Savings _____

Other _____

Paypal _____

Accounts Receivable _____

Current (0-30 Days) _____

31-60 Days _____

61+ Days _____

Action Steps to Collect Money This Week

_____
_____
_____
_____
_____
_____

Priorities for Cash Flow

What will I do with the money I receive?

_____
_____
_____
_____
_____
_____
_____

Date: _____

Liabilities

Credit Card _____

Credit Card _____

Other _____

Loan _____

Accounts Payable _____

Current (0-30 Days) _____

31-60 Days _____

61+ Days _____

Action Steps to Release Money This Week

What bills will I pay?

_____

_____

_____

_____

_____

_____

Upcoming Expenses to Prepare For

_____

_____

_____

_____

_____

_____

Date: _____

Journaling & Notes

How does the big picture of my money make me feel today?

_____
_____
_____
_____
_____
_____

How can I improve my situation?

_____
_____
_____
_____
_____
_____

My money affirmation for this week...

_____
_____
_____
_____
_____
_____

I am grateful for

_____
_____
_____
_____
_____
_____
_____
_____
_____
_____
_____
_____
_____
_____
_____
_____
_____
_____
_____
_____
_____
_____
_____
_____
_____
_____
_____
_____

Date: _____

Assets

Chequing _____

Savings _____

Other _____

Paypal _____

Accounts Receivable _____

Current (0-30 Days) _____

31-60 Days _____

61+ Days _____

Action Steps to Collect Money This Week

_____
_____
_____
_____
_____
_____

Priorities for Cash Flow

What will I do with the money I receive?

_____
_____
_____
_____
_____
_____

Date: _____

Liabilities

Credit Card _____

Credit Card _____

Other _____

Loan _____

Accounts Payable _____

Current (0-30 Days) _____

31-60 Days _____

61+ Days _____

Action Steps to Release Money This Week

What bills will I pay?

_____

_____

_____

_____

_____

_____

Upcoming Expenses to Prepare For

_____

_____

_____

_____

_____

Your MONEYDATE journal

Date: _____

Journaling & Notes

How does the big picture of my money make me feel today?

_____

_____

_____

_____

_____

_____

How can I improve my situation?

_____

_____

_____

_____

_____

_____

My money affirmation for this week...

_____

_____

_____

_____

_____

_____

I am grateful for

Date: _____

REFLECTION

What are you most proud of achieving?	Did you remain in alignment with your money?
What milestones did you bust through? Which ones need to be adjusted?	How did you reward yourself?
Where did you drop the ball? How can you prevent that from happening in the future?	How do you feel about the month overall?

Money rains down on me.

Date: _____

What was your goal for the end of the quarter?

_____
_____
_____
_____
_____

Did you achieve it? What percentage? (divide the actual by the goal $)

_____
_____

How do you feel about your money right now?

_____
_____
_____
_____
_____

What would you like to change or shift?

_____
_____
_____
_____
_____

What can you do to support that change or shift?

_____
_____
_____
_____
_____
_____
_____
_____

What is your goal for the next three months?

_____
_____
_____
_____
_____
_____
_____
_____
_____
_____
_____

Date: _____

Assets

Chequing _____

Savings _____

Other _____

Paypal _____

Accounts Receivable _____

Current (0-30 Days) _____

31-60 Days _____

61+ Days _____

Action Steps to Collect Money This Week

_____

_____

_____

_____

_____

_____

Priorities for Cash Flow

What will I do with the money I receive?

_____

_____

_____

_____

_____

_____

Your MONEYDATE journal

Date: _____

Liabilities

Credit Card _____

Credit Card _____

Other _____

Loan _____

Accounts Payable _____

Current (0-30 Days) _____

31-60 Days _____

61+ Days _____

Action Steps to Release Money This Week

What bills will I pay?

_____

_____

_____

_____

_____

_____

Upcoming Expenses to Prepare For

_____

_____

_____

_____

_____

Date: _____

Journaling & Notes

How does the big picture of my money make me feel today?

_____

_____

_____

_____

_____

How can I improve my situation?

_____

_____

_____

_____

_____

My money affirmation for this week...

_____

_____

_____

_____

_____

I am grateful for

Date: _____

Assets

Chequing _____

Savings _____

Other _____

Paypal _____

Accounts Receivable _____

Current (0-30 Days) _____

31-60 Days _____

61+ Days _____

Action Steps to Collect Money This Week

_____

_____

_____

_____

_____

_____

Priorities for Cash Flow

What will I do with the money I receive?

_____

_____

_____

_____

_____

Date: _____

Liabilities

Credit Card _____

Credit Card _____

Other _____

Loan _____

Accounts Payable _____

   Current (0-30 Days) _____

   31-60 Days _____

   61+ Days _____

Action Steps to Release Money This Week

What bills will I pay?

_____

_____

_____

_____

_____

_____

Upcoming Expenses to Prepare For

_____

_____

_____

_____

_____

_____

Date: _____

Journaling & Notes

How does the big picture of my money make me feel today?

_____

_____

_____

_____

_____

_____

How can I improve my situation?

_____

_____

_____

_____

_____

_____

My money affirmation for this week...

_____

_____

_____

_____

_____

_____

I am grateful for

_____
_____
_____
_____
_____
_____
_____
_____
_____
_____
_____
_____
_____
_____
_____
_____
_____
_____
_____
_____
_____
_____
_____
_____
_____
_____

Date: _____

Assets

Chequing _____

Savings _____

Other _____

Paypal _____

Accounts Receivable _____

Current (0-30 Days) _____

31-60 Days _____

61+ Days _____

Action Steps to Collect Money This Week

_____

_____

_____

_____

_____

_____

Priorities for Cash Flow

What will I do with the money I receive?

_____

_____

_____

_____

_____

_____

Date: _____

Liabilities

Credit Card _____

Credit Card _____

Other _____

Loan _____

Accounts Payable _____

Current (0-30 Days) _____

31-60 Days _____

61+ Days _____

Action Steps to Release Money This Week

What bills will I pay?

_____

_____

_____

_____

_____

_____

Upcoming Expenses to Prepare For

_____

_____

_____

_____

_____

Date: _____

Journaling & Notes

How does the big picture of my money make me feel today?

_____

_____

_____

_____

_____

_____

How can I improve my situation?

_____

_____

_____

_____

_____

_____

My money affirmation for this week...

_____

_____

_____

_____

_____

_____

I am grateful for

Date: _____

Assets

Chequing _____

Savings _____

Other _____

Paypal _____

Accounts Receivable

Current (0-30 Days) _____

31-60 Days _____

61+ Days _____

Action Steps to Collect Money This Week

_____

_____

_____

_____

_____

_____

Priorities for Cash Flow

What will I do with the money I receive?

_____

_____

_____

_____

_____

_____

Date: _____

Liabilities

Credit Card _____

Credit Card _____

Other _____

Loan _____

Accounts Payable _____

Current (0-30 Days) _____

31-60 Days _____

61+ Days _____

Action Steps to Release Money This Week

What bills will I pay?

_____

_____

_____

_____

_____

_____

Upcoming Expenses to Prepare For

_____

_____

_____

_____

_____

Date: _____

Journaling & Notes

How does the big picture of my money make me feel today?

_____
_____
_____
_____
_____

How can I improve my situation?

_____
_____
_____
_____
_____

My money affirmation for this week...

_____
_____
_____
_____
_____

I am grateful for

_____
_____
_____
_____
_____
_____
_____
_____
_____
_____
_____
_____
_____
_____
_____
_____
_____
_____
_____
_____
_____
_____
_____
_____
_____
_____
_____
_____

Date: _____

REFLECTION

What are you most proud of achieving?	Did you remain in alignment with your money?
What milestones did you bust through? Which ones need to be adjusted?	How did you reward yourself?
Where did you drop the ball? How can you prevent that from happening in the future?	How do you feel about the month overall?

I am worthy of money.

Your
MONEYDATE
journal

Date: _____

Assets

Chequing _____

Savings _____

Other _____

Paypal _____

Accounts Receivable

Current (0-30 Days) _____

31-60 Days _____

61+ Days _____

Action Steps to Collect Money This Week

_____

_____

_____

_____

_____

_____

Priorities for Cash Flow

What will I do with the money I receive?

_____

_____

_____

_____

_____

_____

Your MONEY DATE journal

Date: _____

Liabilities

Credit Card _____

Credit Card _____

Other _____

Loan _____

Accounts Payable _____

Current (0-30 Days) _____

31-60 Days _____

61+ Days _____

Action Steps to Release Money This Week

What bills will I pay?

_____

_____

_____

_____

_____

_____

Upcoming Expenses to Prepare For

_____

_____

_____

_____

_____

_____

Date: _____

Journaling & Notes

How does the big picture of my money make me feel today?

_____
_____
_____
_____
_____
_____

How can I improve my situation?

_____
_____
_____
_____
_____
_____

My money affirmation for this week...

_____
_____
_____
_____
_____
_____

I am grateful for

_____
_____
_____
_____
_____
_____
_____
_____
_____
_____
_____
_____
_____
_____
_____
_____
_____
_____
_____
_____
_____
_____
_____
_____
_____
_____
_____
_____
_____
_____
_____

Date: _____

Assets

Chequing _____

Savings _____

Other _____

Paypal _____

Accounts Receivable

Current (0-30 Days) _____

31-60 Days _____

61+ Days _____

Action Steps to Collect Money This Week

_____

_____

_____

_____

_____

Priorities for Cash Flow

What will I do with the money I receive?

_____

_____

_____

_____

_____

_____

Date: _____

Liabilities

Credit Card _____

Credit Card _____

Other _____

Loan _____

Accounts Payable _____

   Current (0-30 Days) _____

   31-60 Days _____

   61+ Days _____

Action Steps to Release Money This Week

What bills will I pay?

_____

_____

_____

_____

_____

_____

Upcoming Expenses to Prepare For

_____

_____

_____

_____

_____

_____

Your MONEYDATE journal

Date: _____

Journaling & Notes

How does the big picture of my money make me feel today?

_____
_____
_____
_____
_____
_____

How can I improve my situation?

_____
_____
_____
_____
_____
_____

My money affirmation for this week...

_____
_____
_____
_____
_____
_____

I am grateful for

_____
_____
_____
_____
_____
_____
_____
_____
_____
_____
_____
_____
_____
_____
_____
_____
_____
_____
_____
_____
_____
_____
_____
_____
_____
_____
_____
_____
_____
_____
_____
_____
_____

Date: _____

Assets

Chequing _____

Savings _____

Other _____

Paypal _____

Accounts Receivable _____

Current (0-30 Days) _____

31-60 Days _____

61+ Days _____

Action Steps to Collect Money This Week

_____

_____

_____

_____

_____

_____

Priorities for Cash Flow

What will I do with the money I receive?

_____

_____

_____

_____

_____

_____

Date: _____

Liabilities

Credit Card _____

Credit Card _____

Other _____

Loan _____

Accounts Payable _____

    Current (0-30 Days) _____

    31-60 Days _____

    61+ Days _____

Action Steps to Release Money This Week

What bills will I pay?

_____

_____

_____

_____

_____

_____

Upcoming Expenses to Prepare For

_____

_____

_____

_____

_____

_____

Your MONEY DATE journal

Date: _____

Journaling & Notes

How does the big picture of my money make me feel today?

_____
_____
_____
_____
_____
_____

How can I improve my situation?

_____
_____
_____
_____
_____
_____

My money affirmation for this week...

_____
_____
_____
_____
_____
_____

I am grateful for

Your MONEYDATE journal

Date: _____

Assets

Chequing _____

Savings _____

Other _____

Paypal _____

Accounts Receivable _____

Current (0-30 Days) _____

31-60 Days _____

61+ Days _____

Action Steps to Collect Money This Week

_____

_____

_____

_____

_____

_____

Priorities for Cash Flow

What will I do with the money I receive?

_____

_____

_____

_____

_____

_____

Date: _____

Liabilities

Credit Card _____

Credit Card _____

Other _____

Loan _____

Accounts Payable _____

Current (0-30 Days) _____

31-60 Days _____

61+ Days _____

Action Steps to Release Money This Week

What bills will I pay?

_____

_____

_____

_____

_____

_____

Upcoming Expenses to Prepare For

_____

_____

_____

_____

_____

_____

Your MONEYDATE journal

Date: _____

Journaling & Notes

How does the big picture of my money make me feel today?

_____
_____
_____
_____
_____

How can I improve my situation?

_____
_____
_____
_____
_____

My money affirmation for this week...

_____
_____
_____
_____
_____

I am grateful for

_____
_____
_____
_____
_____
_____
_____
_____
_____
_____
_____
_____
_____
_____
_____
_____
_____
_____
_____
_____
_____
_____
_____
_____
_____
_____
_____
_____
_____

Date: _____

REFLECTION

What are you most proud of achieving?	Did you remain in alignment with your money?
What milestones did you bust through? Which ones need to be adjusted?	How did you reward yourself?
Where did you drop the ball? How can you prevent that from happening in the future?	How do you feel about the month overall?

I live in the sacred flow of money.

Date: _____

Assets

Chequing _____

Savings _____

Other _____

Paypal _____

Accounts Receivable _____

Current (0-30 Days) _____

31-60 Days _____

61+ Days _____

Action Steps to Collect Money This Week

_____
_____
_____
_____
_____
_____

Priorities for Cash Flow

What will I do with the money I receive?

_____
_____
_____
_____
_____
_____

Your MONEYDATE journal

Date: _____

Liabilities

Credit Card _____

Credit Card _____

Other _____

Loan _____

Accounts Payable _____

Current (0-30 Days) _____

31-60 Days _____

61+ Days _____

Action Steps to Release Money This Week

What bills will I pay?

_____

_____

_____

_____

_____

_____

Upcoming Expenses to Prepare For

_____

_____

_____

_____

_____

_____

Date: _____

Journaling & Notes

How does the big picture of my money make me feel today?

_____
_____
_____
_____
_____

How can I improve my situation?

_____
_____
_____
_____
_____

My money affirmation for this week...

_____
_____
_____
_____
_____

I am grateful for

Your
MONEYDATE
journal

Date: _____

Assets

Chequing _____

Savings _____

Other _____

Paypal _____

Accounts Receivable _____

Current (0-30 Days) _____

31-60 Days _____

61+ Days _____

Action Steps to Collect Money This Week

_____

_____

_____

_____

_____

Priorities for Cash Flow

What will I do with the money I receive?

_____

_____

_____

_____

_____

Date: _____

Liabilities

Credit Card _____

Credit Card _____

Other _____

Loan _____

Accounts Payable _____

    Current (0-30 Days) _____

    31-60 Days _____

    61+ Days _____

Action Steps to Release Money This Week

What bills will I pay?

_____

_____

_____

_____

_____

_____

Upcoming Expenses to Prepare For

_____

_____

_____

_____

_____

_____

Date: _____

Journaling & Notes

How does the big picture of my money make me feel today?

_____
_____
_____
_____
_____
_____

How can I improve my situation?

_____
_____
_____
_____
_____

My money affirmation for this week...

_____
_____
_____
_____
_____

I am grateful for

_____
_____
_____
_____
_____
_____
_____
_____
_____
_____
_____
_____
_____
_____
_____
_____
_____
_____
_____
_____
_____
_____
_____
_____
_____
_____
_____
_____
_____

Your MONEYDATE journal

Date: _____

Assets

Chequing _____

Savings _____

Other _____

Paypal _____

Accounts Receivable

Current (0-30 Days) _____

31-60 Days _____

61+ Days _____

Action Steps to Collect Money This Week

_____

_____

_____

_____

_____

_____

Priorities for Cash Flow

What will I do with the money I receive?

_____

_____

_____

_____

_____

_____

Date: _____

Liabilities

Credit Card _____

Credit Card _____

Other _____

Loan _____

Accounts Payable _____

Current (0-30 Days) _____

31-60 Days _____

61+ Days _____

Action Steps to Release Money This Week

What bills will I pay?

_____

_____

_____

_____

_____

_____

Upcoming Expenses to Prepare For

_____

_____

_____

_____

_____

_____

Date: _____

Journaling & Notes

How does the big picture of my money make me feel today?

_____
_____
_____
_____
_____
_____

How can I improve my situation?

_____
_____
_____
_____
_____
_____

My money affirmation for this week...

_____
_____
_____
_____
_____
_____

I am grateful for

_____

_____

_____

_____

_____

_____

_____

_____

_____

_____

_____

_____

_____

_____

_____

_____

_____

_____

_____

_____

_____

_____

_____

_____

_____

_____

_____

_____

Date: _____

Assets

Chequing _____

Savings _____

Other _____

Paypal _____

Accounts Receivable

Current (0-30 Days) _____

31-60 Days _____

61+ Days _____

Action Steps to Collect Money This Week

_____

_____

_____

_____

_____

_____

Priorities for Cash Flow

What will I do with the money I receive?

_____

_____

_____

_____

_____

_____

Date: _____

Liabilities

Credit Card _____

Credit Card _____

Other _____

Loan _____

Accounts Payable _____

Current (0-30 Days) _____

31-60 Days _____

61+ Days _____

Action Steps to Release Money This Week

What bills will I pay?

_____

_____

_____

_____

_____

_____

Upcoming Expenses to Prepare For

_____

_____

_____

_____

_____

_____

Your
MONEYDATE *journal*

Date: _____

Journaling & Notes

How does the big picture of my money make me feel today?

_____
_____
_____
_____
_____

How can I improve my situation?

_____
_____
_____
_____
_____
_____

My money affirmation for this week...

_____
_____
_____
_____
_____
_____

I am grateful for

_____

_____

_____

_____

_____

_____

_____

_____

_____

_____

_____

_____

_____

_____

_____

_____

_____

_____

_____

_____

_____

_____

_____

_____

_____

_____

_____

Date: _____

REFLECTION

What are you most proud of achieving?	Did you remain in alignment with your money?
What milestones did you bust through? Which ones need to be adjusted?	**How did you reward yourself?**
Where did you drop the ball? How can you prevent that from happening in the future?	**How do you feel about the month overall?**

I release my attachment to what wealthy looks like.

Date: _____

What was your goal for the end of the quarter?

_____
_____
_____
_____
_____

Did you achieve it? What percentage? (divide the actual by the goal $)

_____
_____
_____

How do you feel about your money right now?

_____
_____
_____
_____
_____

What would you like to change or shift?

_____
_____
_____
_____
_____

What can you do to support that change or shift?

_____
_____
_____
_____
_____
_____
_____
_____

What is your goal for the next three months?

_____
_____
_____
_____
_____
_____
_____
_____
_____
_____

Your MONEY DATE journal

Date: _____

Assets

Chequing _____

Savings _____

Other _____

Paypal _____

Accounts Receivable _____

Current (0-30 Days) _____

31-60 Days _____

61+ Days _____

Action Steps to Collect Money This Week

_____

_____

_____

_____

_____

_____

Priorities for Cash Flow

What will I do with the money I receive?

_____

_____

_____

_____

_____

_____

Date: _____

Liabilities

Credit Card _____

Credit Card _____

Other _____

Loan _____

Accounts Payable _____

Current (0-30 Days) _____

31-60 Days _____

61+ Days _____

Action Steps to Release Money This Week

What bills will I pay?

_____

_____

_____

_____

_____

_____

Upcoming Expenses to Prepare For

_____

_____

_____

_____

_____

_____

Your
MONEY DATE
journal

Date: _____

Journaling & Notes

How does the big picture of my money make me feel today?

_____
_____
_____
_____
_____
_____

How can I improve my situation?

_____
_____
_____
_____
_____
_____

My money affirmation for this week...

_____
_____
_____
_____
_____
_____

I am grateful for

_____
_____
_____
_____
_____
_____
_____
_____
_____
_____
_____
_____
_____
_____
_____
_____
_____
_____
_____
_____
_____
_____
_____
_____
_____
_____
_____
_____
_____
_____

Date: _____

Assets

Chequing _____

Savings _____

Other _____

Paypal _____

Accounts Receivable _____

Current (0-30 Days) _____

31-60 Days _____

61+ Days _____

Action Steps to Collect Money This Week

_____

_____

_____

_____

_____

_____

Priorities for Cash Flow

What will I do with the money I receive?

_____

_____

_____

_____

_____

_____

Date: _____

Liabilities

Credit Card _____

Credit Card _____

Other _____

Loan _____

Accounts Payable _____

   Current (0-30 Days) _____

   31-60 Days _____

   61+ Days _____

Action Steps to Release Money This Week

What bills will I pay?

_____

_____

_____

_____

_____

_____

Upcoming Expenses to Prepare For

_____

_____

_____

_____

_____

_____

Date: _____

Journaling & Notes

How does the big picture of my money make me feel today?

_____
_____
_____
_____
_____
_____

How can I improve my situation?

_____
_____
_____
_____
_____
_____

My money affirmation for this week...

_____
_____
_____
_____
_____
_____

I am grateful for

_____
_____
_____
_____
_____
_____
_____
_____
_____
_____
_____
_____
_____
_____
_____
_____
_____
_____
_____
_____
_____
_____
_____
_____
_____
_____
_____
_____

Your
MONEYDATE
journal

Date: _____

Assets

Chequing _____

Savings _____

Other _____

Paypal _____

Accounts Receivable _____

Current (0-30 Days) _____

31-60 Days _____

61+ Days _____

Action Steps to Collect Money This Week

_____
_____
_____
_____
_____
_____

Priorities for Cash Flow

What will I do with the money I receive?

_____
_____
_____
_____
_____

Your MONEYDATE journal

Date: _____

Liabilities

Credit Card _____

Credit Card _____

Other _____

Loan _____

Accounts Payable _____

Current (0-30 Days) _____

31-60 Days _____

61+ Days _____

Action Steps to Release Money This Week

What bills will I pay?

_____

_____

_____

_____

_____

_____

Upcoming Expenses to Prepare For

_____

_____

_____

_____

_____

_____

Date: _____

Journaling & Notes

How does the big picture of my money make me feel today?

_____
_____
_____
_____
_____
_____

How can I improve my situation?

_____
_____
_____
_____
_____
_____

My money affirmation for this week...

_____
_____
_____
_____
_____
_____

I am grateful for

_____
_____
_____
_____
_____
_____
_____
_____
_____
_____
_____
_____
_____
_____
_____
_____
_____
_____
_____
_____
_____
_____
_____
_____
_____
_____
_____
_____

Date: _____

Assets

Chequing _____

Savings _____

Other _____

Paypal _____

Accounts Receivable _____

Current (0-30 Days) _____

31-60 Days _____

61+ Days _____

Action Steps to Collect Money This Week

_____

_____

_____

_____

_____

_____

Priorities for Cash Flow

What will I do with the money I receive?

_____

_____

_____

_____

_____

_____

Date: _____

Liabilities

Credit Card _____

Credit Card _____

Other _____

Loan _____

Accounts Payable _____

 Current (0-30 Days) _____

 31-60 Days _____

 61+ Days _____

Action Steps to Release Money This Week

What bills will I pay?

_____

_____

_____

_____

_____

_____

Upcoming Expenses to Prepare For

_____

_____

_____

_____

_____

_____

Your MONEYDATE journal

Date: _____

Journaling & Notes

How does the big picture of my money make me feel today?

_____

_____

_____

_____

_____

_____

How can I improve my situation?

_____

_____

_____

_____

_____

_____

My money affirmation for this week...

_____

_____

_____

_____

_____

_____

I am grateful for

_____
_____
_____
_____
_____
_____
_____
_____
_____
_____
_____
_____
_____
_____
_____
_____
_____
_____
_____
_____
_____
_____
_____
_____
_____
_____
_____
_____
_____

Date: _____

REFLECTION

What are you most proud of achieving?	Did you remain in alignment with your money?
What milestones did you bust through? Which ones need to be adjusted?	How did you reward yourself?
Where did you drop the ball? How can you prevent that from happening in the future?	How do you feel about the month overall?

Positive Money Affirmation

I receive money with gratitude.

Date: _____

Assets

Chequing _____

Savings _____

Other _____

Paypal _____

Accounts Receivable _____

Current (0-30 Days) _____

31-60 Days _____

61+ Days _____

Action Steps to Collect Money This Week

_____

_____

_____

_____

_____

_____

Priorities for Cash Flow

What will I do with the money I receive?

_____

_____

_____

_____

_____

_____

Your MONEY DATE journal

Date: _____

Liabilities

Credit Card _____

Credit Card _____

Other _____

Loan _____

Accounts Payable _____

Current (0-30 Days) _____

31-60 Days _____

61+ Days _____

Action Steps to Release Money This Week

What bills will I pay?

_____

_____

_____

_____

_____

_____

Upcoming Expenses to Prepare For

_____

_____

_____

_____

_____

_____

Date: _____

Journaling & Notes

How does the big picture of my money make me feel today?

_____
_____
_____
_____
_____
_____

How can I improve my situation?

_____
_____
_____
_____
_____
_____

My money affirmation for this week...

_____
_____
_____
_____
_____
_____

I am grateful for

Your MONEYDATE journal

Date: _____

Assets

Chequing _____

Savings _____

Other _____

Paypal _____

Accounts Receivable _____

Current (0-30 Days) _____

31-60 Days _____

61+ Days _____

Action Steps to Collect Money This Week

_____

_____

_____

_____

_____

_____

Priorities for Cash Flow

What will I do with the money I receive?

_____

_____

_____

_____

_____

_____

Date: _____

Liabilities

Credit Card _____

Credit Card _____

Other _____

Loan _____

Accounts Payable _____

    Current (0-30 Days) _____

    31-60 Days _____

    61+ Days _____

Action Steps to Release Money This Week

What bills will I pay?

_____

_____

_____

_____

_____

_____

Upcoming Expenses to Prepare For

_____

_____

_____

_____

_____

_____

Date: _____

Journaling & Notes

How does the big picture of my money make me feel today?

_____
_____
_____
_____
_____
_____

How can I improve my situation?

_____
_____
_____
_____
_____
_____

My money affirmation for this week...

_____
_____
_____
_____
_____
_____

I am grateful for

_____
_____
_____
_____
_____
_____
_____
_____
_____
_____
_____
_____
_____
_____
_____
_____
_____
_____
_____
_____
_____
_____
_____
_____
_____
_____
_____
_____
_____

Date: _____

Assets

Chequing _____

Savings _____

Other _____

Paypal _____

Accounts Receivable _____

Current (0-30 Days) _____

31-60 Days _____

61+ Days _____

Action Steps to Collect Money This Week

_____

_____

_____

_____

_____

_____

Priorities for Cash Flow

What will I do with the money I receive?

_____

_____

_____

_____

_____

_____

Date: _____

Liabilities

Credit Card _____

Credit Card _____

Other _____

Loan _____

Accounts Payable _____

    Current (0-30 Days) _____

    31-60 Days _____

    61+ Days _____

Action Steps to Release Money This Week

What bills will I pay?

_____

_____

_____

_____

_____

_____

Upcoming Expenses to Prepare For

_____

_____

_____

_____

_____

_____

Date: _____

Journaling & Notes

How does the big picture of my money make me feel today?

_____
_____
_____
_____
_____
_____

How can I improve my situation?

_____
_____
_____
_____
_____
_____

My money affirmation for this week...

_____
_____
_____
_____
_____
_____

I am grateful for

Date: _____

Assets

Chequing _____

Savings _____

Other _____

Paypal _____

Accounts Receivable _____

Current (0-30 Days) _____

31-60 Days _____

61+ Days _____

Action Steps to Collect Money This Week

_____
_____
_____
_____
_____
_____

Priorities for Cash Flow

What will I do with the money I receive?

_____
_____
_____
_____
_____
_____

Date: _____

Liabilities

Credit Card _____

Credit Card _____

Other _____

Loan _____

Accounts Payable _____

    Current (0-30 Days) _____

    31-60 Days _____

    61+ Days _____

Action Steps to Release Money This Week

What bills will I pay?

_____

_____

_____

_____

_____

_____

Upcoming Expenses to Prepare For

_____

_____

_____

_____

_____

_____

Your MONEYDATE journal

Date: _____

Journaling & Notes

How does the big picture of my money make me feel today?

_____
_____
_____
_____
_____
_____

How can I improve my situation?

_____
_____
_____
_____
_____

My money affirmation for this week…

_____
_____
_____
_____
_____
_____

I am grateful for

_____

_____

_____

_____

_____

_____

_____

_____

_____

_____

_____

_____

_____

_____

_____

_____

_____

_____

_____

_____

_____

_____

_____

_____

_____

_____

_____

_____

Date: _____

REFLECTION

What are you most proud of achieving?	Did you remain in alignment with your money?
What milestones did you bust through? Which ones need to be adjusted?	How did you reward yourself?
Where did you drop the ball? How can you prevent that from happening in the future?	How do you feel about the month overall?

Wealth is a mindset.

Date: _____

Assets

Chequing _____

Savings _____

Other _____

Paypal _____

Accounts Receivable _____

Current (0-30 Days) _____

31-60 Days _____

61+ Days _____

Action Steps to Collect Money This Week

_____

_____

_____

_____

_____

_____

Priorities for Cash Flow

What will I do with the money I receive?

_____

_____

_____

_____

_____

_____

Your
MONEYDATE
journal

Date: _____

Liabilities

Credit Card _____

Credit Card _____

Other _____

Loan _____

Accounts Payable _____

　　Current (0-30 Days) _____

　31-60 Days _____

　61+ Days _____

Action Steps to Release Money This Week

What bills will I pay?

_____

_____

_____

_____

_____

_____

Upcoming Expenses to Prepare For

_____

_____

_____

_____

_____

_____

Date: _____

Journaling & Notes

How does the big picture of my money make me feel today?

_____
_____
_____
_____
_____
_____

How can I improve my situation?

_____
_____
_____
_____
_____
_____

My money affirmation for this week...

_____
_____
_____
_____
_____
_____

I am grateful for

_____
_____
_____
_____
_____
_____
_____
_____
_____
_____
_____
_____
_____
_____
_____
_____
_____
_____
_____
_____
_____
_____
_____
_____
_____
_____
_____
_____

Date: _____

Assets

Chequing _____

Savings _____

Other _____

Paypal _____

Accounts Receivable _____

Current (0-30 Days) _____

31-60 Days _____

61+ Days _____

Action Steps to Collect Money This Week

_____

_____

_____

_____

_____

_____

Priorities for Cash Flow

What will I do with the money I receive?

_____

_____

_____

_____

_____

_____

Your
MONEYDATE *journal*

Date: _____

Liabilities

Credit Card _____
Credit Card _____
Other _____
Loan _____
Accounts Payable _____

   Current (0-30 Days) _____
   31-60 Days _____
   61+ Days _____

Action Steps to Release Money This Week

What bills will I pay?

_____
_____
_____
_____
_____
_____

Upcoming Expenses to Prepare For

_____
_____
_____
_____
_____
_____

Date: _____

Journaling & Notes

How does the big picture of my money make me feel today?

_____
_____
_____
_____
_____

How can I improve my situation?

_____
_____
_____
_____
_____
_____

My money affirmation for this week...

_____
_____
_____
_____
_____

I am grateful for

_____
_____
_____
_____
_____
_____
_____
_____
_____
_____
_____
_____
_____
_____
_____
_____
_____
_____
_____
_____
_____
_____
_____
_____
_____
_____
_____
_____

Date: _____

Assets

Chequing _____

Savings _____

Other _____

Paypal _____

Accounts Receivable _____

Current (0-30 Days) _____

31-60 Days _____

61+ Days _____

Action Steps to Collect Money This Week

_____

_____

_____

_____

_____

_____

Priorities for Cash Flow

What will I do with the money I receive?

_____

_____

_____

_____

_____

_____

Date: _____

Liabilities

Credit Card _____

Credit Card _____

Other _____

Loan _____

Accounts Payable _____

Current (0-30 Days) _____

31-60 Days _____

61+ Days _____

Action Steps to Release Money This Week

What bills will I pay?

_____

_____

_____

_____

_____

_____

Upcoming Expenses to Prepare For

_____

_____

_____

_____

_____

_____

Your
MONEYDATE
journal

Date: _____

Journaling & Notes

How does the big picture of my money make me feel today?

_____
_____
_____
_____
_____
_____

How can I improve my situation?

_____
_____
_____
_____
_____
_____

My money affirmation for this week...

_____
_____
_____
_____
_____
_____

I am grateful for

Date: _____

Assets

Chequing _____

Savings _____

Other _____

Paypal _____

Accounts Receivable _____

Current (0-30 Days) _____

31-60 Days _____

61+ Days _____

Action Steps to Collect Money This Week

_____

_____

_____

_____

_____

_____

Priorities for Cash Flow

What will I do with the money I receive?

_____

_____

_____

_____

_____

_____

Date: _____

Liabilities

Credit Card _____

Credit Card _____

Other _____

Loan _____

Accounts Payable _____

Current (0-30 Days) _____

31-60 Days _____

61+ Days _____

Action Steps to Release Money This Week

What bills will I pay?

_____

_____

_____

_____

_____

_____

Upcoming Expenses to Prepare For

_____

_____

_____

_____

_____

_____

Date: _____

Journaling & Notes

How does the big picture of my money make me feel today?

_____
_____
_____
_____
_____
_____

How can I improve my situation?

_____
_____
_____
_____
_____
_____

My money affirmation for this week...

_____
_____
_____
_____
_____
_____

I am grateful for

_____
_____
_____
_____
_____
_____
_____
_____
_____
_____
_____
_____
_____
_____
_____
_____
_____
_____
_____
_____
_____
_____
_____
_____
_____
_____
_____

Date: _____

REFLECTION

What are you most proud of achieving?	Did you remain in alignment with your money?
What milestones did you bust through? Which ones need to be adjusted?	How did you reward yourself?
Where did you drop the ball? How can you prevent that from happening in the future?	How do you feel about the month overall?

I release my attachment to what wealthy looks like.

Date: _____

What was your goal for the end of the quarter?

_____
_____
_____
_____
_____
_____

Did you achieve it? What percentage? (divide the actual by the goal $)

_____
_____
_____

How do you feel about your money right now?

_____
_____
_____
_____
_____

What would you like to change or shift?

_____
_____
_____
_____
_____

What can you do to support that change or shift?

_____
_____
_____
_____
_____
_____
_____
_____
_____

What is your goal for the next three months?

_____
_____
_____
_____
_____
_____
_____
_____
_____
_____
_____

You Did It!

You Did it! When we come to the end of a journey, you may think we're done, but the truth is, you just got started!

I hope that this process becomes a lifelong habit and ritual – a luxurious time that you spend with your money as you co-create your wealth, your abundance, and your awesome life.

I don't see this as an end at all; I see it as a jump-off point for an even higher level up. I invite you to take some time to congratulate yourself and celebrate.

YOU DID IT! All of it! You did the work, and you have reaped the rewards. Congratulations! Thank you for believing in yourself. Thank you for committing to your money, for showing up and doing the work. Thank you for what you and your money are contributing to our world.

What happens next? I recommend you do something EPIC! Really reward yourself. You have achieved A LOT. Then I suggest you do a little review – what happened, what worked, when did you get sidetracked, how did you stay on task? Acknowledge it. Let it all sink in. You may have come very far, but you may be able to go further. Learn from your journey and continue building momentum.

Pick up a new copy of *Your MoneyDate Journal* for your next fifty-two weeks of wealth, building on the powerful habits you have already created. Can you imagine your life at this time next year?

Wow! It is my honour to support you in achieving your money dreams.

With gratitude,

Michelle

About the Author

Growing up on the West Coast of Canada, Michelle learned at an early age that money equaled hard work and sacrifice. As she watched her father and brothers work physically hard to earn money in the commercial fishing industry, she adopted that same attitude. It has to be a struggle, there has to be sacrifice – and if it doesn't feel that way, well damn well make it feel that way – so she becomes an over-achiever.

Justifying her pay cheque by working long hours, dedicated to her job, over delivering for her pay cheque. Well, that only gets you so far. The same became true when she started her own business – those limiting beliefs kicked in and she found herself in the same position but with herself as the "boss".

It became clear to Michelle that there was a missing piece to this puzzle of money. She found herself creating the most amazing strategic financial growth plans for her clients, but often that didn't matter because their own limiting beliefs took over and they continued to struggle. This is where self-discovery kicked in for Michelle. She spent many years learning about limiting beliefs, meditation, trust, intuition, our higher power, and all the practices that go alongside to support growth and abundance.

And this is where the magic happened. Michelle realized that she had a unique insight and ability to marry the masculine and feminine energy of money and support people to bring all kinds of abundance into their lives – especially money. This felt like an incredible gift she had been given and she had a responsibility to share it with the world.

Connect with Michelle:

www.michellecooper-author.com
www.facebook.com/AuthorMichelleCooper/
Instagram: @michellebcooper

Other Books and Programs by Michelle

Follow Michelle on Amazon and learn about her upcoming books.
amazon.com/author/michellecooper

Join her Facebook Communities and make use of her free resources!

The Vault - Facebook Group
www.facebook.com/groups/thebusinessvault/

Your MoneyDate Facebook Group
www.facebook.com/groups/MoneyDate/

Bonus GIfts!
michellebcooper.com/money-date-bonuses

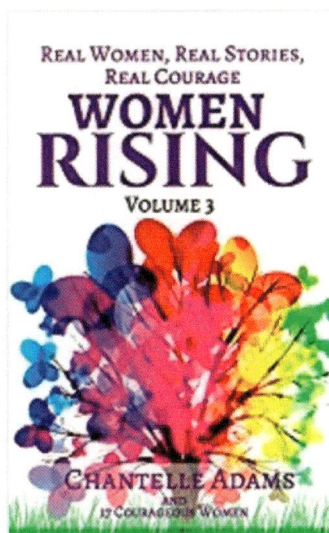

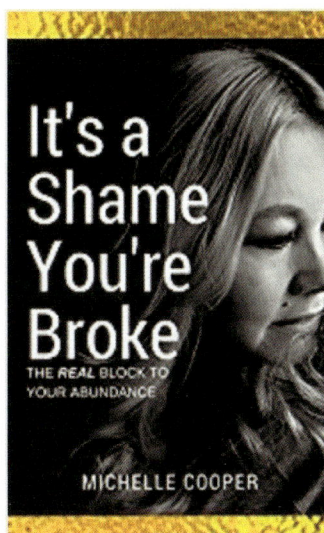

REAL WOMEN, REAL STORIES, REAL COURAGE
WOMEN RISING
VOLUME 3
CHANTELLE ADAMS
AND 17 COURAGEOUS WOMEN

It's a Shame You're Broke
THE REAL BLOCK TO YOUR ABUNDANCE
MICHELLE COOPER

Made in the USA
Columbia, SC
10 February 2018